I SAID THAT LOVE
HEALS FROM INSIDE

T0201777

A Wesleyan Chapbook

I SAID THAT LOVE HEALS FROM INSIDE

Love Poems of
Yusef Komunyakaa

Edited by Oliver Egger

Wesleyan University Press
Middletown, Connecticut

Wesleyan University Press
Middletown Connecticut 06459
www.weslpress.org

ISBN 978-0-8195-0167-7

Cover Image: ***Odysseus Leaves Circe***
by Romare Bearden. © 2024 Romare
Bearden Foundation / Licensed by VAGA
at Artists Rights Society (ARS), NY.

CONTENTS

Note to the Reader

Dear Reader,

Thank you for picking up this little book of love poems.
Wesleyan University Press and Yusef Komunyakaa have
been working together since 1984 with the publication of
Copacetic. Komunyakaa eventually published nine books
with Wesleyan, including the 1993 Pulitzer Prize-winning
collection, *Neon Vernacular: New and Selected Poems.*

This chapbook is a companion to *Dear Yusef: Essays,
Letters, and Poems, For and About One Mr. Komunyakaa,*
edited by John Murillo and Nicole Sealey. It includes poems
from Komunyakaa's Wesleyan books, and several from his
later volumes.

This collection embraces a broad understanding of the love
poem. Indeed, to put together a collection of love poems
is to come to terms with how love or its absence permeates
everything. As Mr. Komunyakaa writes to conclude the
poem "Copacetic Mingus", in the end every song is saying
the same thing: "Hard love, it's hard love."

—*Oliver Egger*

Corrigenda

I take it back.
The crow doesn't have red wings.
They're pages of dust.
The woman in the dark room
takes the barrel of a .357 magnum
out of her mouth, reclines
on your bed, a Helena Rubinstein smile.
I'm sorry, you won't know your father
by his darksome old clothes.
He won't be standing by that tree.
I haven't salted the tail
of the sparrow.
Erase its song from this page.
I haven't seen the moon
fall open at the golden edge of our sleep.
I haven't been there
like the tumor in each of us.
There's no death that can
hold us together like twin brothers
coming home to bury their mother.
I never said there's a book inside
every tree. I never said I know how
the legless beggar feels when
the memory of his toes itch.
If I did, drunkenness
was then my god & naked dancer.
I take it back.
I'm not a suicidal mooncalf;
you don't have to take my shoelaces.
If you must quote me, remember
I said that love heals from inside.

For You, Sweetheart, I'll Sell Plutonium Reactors

For you, sweetheart, I'll ride back down
into black smoke early Sunday morning
cutting fog, grab the moneysack
of gold teeth. Diamond mines
soil creep groan ancient cities, archaeological
diggings, & yellow bulldozers turn around all night
in blood-lit villages. Inhabitants here once gathered seashells
that glimmered like pearls. When the smoke clears, you'll see
an erected throne like a mountain to scale,
institutions built with bones, guns hidden in walls
that swing open like big-mouthed B-52s.
Your face in the mirror is my face. You tapdance
on tabletops for me, while corporate bosses
arm wrestle in back rooms for your essential downfall.
I entice homosexuals into my basement butcher shop.
I put my hands around another sharecropper's throat
for that mink coat you want from Saks Fifth,
short-change another beggarwoman,
steal another hit song from Sleepy
John Estes, salt another gold mine in Cripple Creek,
drive another motorcycle up a circular ice wall,
face another public gunslinger like a bad chest wound,
just to slide hands under black silk.
Like the Ancient Mariner steering a skeleton ship
against the moon, I'm their hired gunman
if the price is right, take a contract on myself.
They'll name mountains & rivers in my honor.
I'm a drawbridge over manholes for you, sweetheart.
I'm paid two hundred grand
to pick up a red telephone anytime & call up God.
I'm making tobacco pouches out of the breasts of Indian
maidens so we can stand in a valley & watch grass grow.

Unnatural State of the Unicorn

Introduce me first as a man.
Don't mention superficial laurels
the dead heap up on the living.
I am a man. Cut me & I bleed.
Before embossed limited editions,
before fat artichoke hearts marinated
in rich sauce & served with imported wines,
before antics & Agnus Dei,
before the stars in your eyes
mean birth sign or Impression,
I am a man. I've scuffled
in mudholes, broken teeth in a grinning skull
like the moon behind bars. I've done it all
to be known as myself. No titles.
I have principles. I won't speak
on the natural state of the unicorn
in literature or self-analysis.
I have no birthright to prove,
no insignia, no secret
password, no fleur-de-lis.
My initials aren't on a branding iron.
I'm standing here in unpolished
shoes & faded jeans, sweating
my manly sweat. Inside my skin,
loving you, I am this space
my body believes in.

Copacetic Mingus

"'Mingus One, Two and Three.
Which is the image you want the world to see?'"
—Charles Mingus, *Beneath the Underdog*

Heartstring. Blessed wood
& every moment the thing's made of:
ball of fatback
licked by fingers of fire.
Hard love, it's hard love.
Running big hands down
the upright's wide hips,
rocking his moon-eyed mistress
with gold in her teeth.
Art & life bleed
into each other
as he works the bow.
But tonight we're both a long ways
from the Mile High City,
1973. Here in New Orleans
years below sea level,
I listen to *Pithecanthropus*
Erectus: Up & down, under
& over, every which way—
thump, thump, dada—ah, yes.
Wood heavy with tenderness,
Mingus fingers the loom
gone on Segovia,
dogging the raw strings
unwaxed with rosin.
Hyperbolic bass line. Oh, no!
Hard love, it's hard love.

Banking Potatoes

Daddy would drop purple-veined vines
Along rows of dark loam
& I'd march behind him
Like a peg-legged soldier,
Pushing down the stick
With a V cut into its tip.

Three weeks before the first frost
I'd follow his horse-drawn plow
That opened up the soil & left
Sweet potatoes sticky with sap,
Like flesh-colored stones along a riverbed
Or diminished souls beside a mass grave.

They lay all day under the sun's
Invisible weight, & by twilight
We'd bury them under pine needles
& then shovel in two feet of dirt.
Nighthawks scalloped the sweaty air,
Their wings spread wide

As plowshares. But soon the wind
Knocked on doors & windows
Like a frightened stranger,
& by mid-winter we had tunneled
Back into the tomb of straw,
Unable to divide love from hunger.

Reminiscence

I had brainphotos
of riding you down into music.
I tried to kiss you back then,
but didn't know the sweet punishment
of a tongue inside another voice.
You were a tree breaking with mangoes,
bent toward deeper earth,
& ran out into the world
before me. Songs floated ahead
like comic-strip balloons
where they could breathe hard
& blow dreams apart.

The green light kept going
beyond Blueberry Hill.
Bandages of silence
didn't conceal unsolved crimes,
& I deserted my voice crawling
over cobblestone.
My ribcage a harp
for many fingers.
I've seen overturned deathcarts
with their wheels churning
Guadalajara mornings,
but your face will always be
a private country.

Euphony

Hands make love to thigh, breast, clavicle,
Willed to each other, to the keyboard—
Searching the whole forest of compromises
Till the soft engine kicks in, running

On honey. Dissonance worked
Into harmony, evenhanded
As Art Tatum's plea to the keys.
Like a woman & man who have lived

A long time together, they know how
To keep the song alive. Wordless
Epics into the cold night, keepers
Of the fire—the right hand lifts

Like the ghost of a sparrow
& the left uses every motionless muscle.
Notes divide, balancing each other,
Love & hate tattooed on the fingers.

Providence

I walked away with your face
stolen from a crowded room,
& the sting of requited memory
lived beneath my skin. A name
raw on my tongue, in my brain, a glimpse
nestled years later like a red bird
among wet leaves on a dull day.

A face. The tilt of a head. Dark
lipstick. *Aletheia.* The unknown
marked on a shoulder, night
weather in our heads.
I pushed out of this half-stunned
yes, begging light, beyond the caul's
shadow, dangling the lifeline of Oh.

I took seven roads to get here
& almost died three times.
How many near misses before
new days slouched into the left corner
pocket, before the hanging fruit
made me kneel? I crossed
five times in the blood to see

the plots against the future—
 descendent of a house that knows
all my strong & weak points.
No bounty of love apples glistened
with sweat, a pear-shaped lute
plucked in the valley of the tuber rose
& Madonna lily. Your name untied

every knot in my body, a honey-eating
animal reflected in shop windows
& twinned against this underworld.
Out of tide-lull & upwash
a perfect hunger slipped in
tooled by an eye, & this morning
makes us the oldest song in any god's throat.

We had gone back walking
on our hands. Opened by a kiss,
by fingertips on the Abyssinian
stem & nape, we bloomed
from underneath stone. Moon-pulled
fish skirted the gangplank,
a dung-scented ark of gopherwood.

Now, you are on my skin, in my mouth
& hair as if you were always
woven in my walk, a rib
unearthed like a necklace of sand dollars
out of black hush. You are a call
& response going back to the first
praise-lament, the old wish

made flesh. The two of us
a third voice, an incantation
sweet-talked & grunted out of The Hawk's
midnight horn. I have you inside
a hard question, & it won't let go,
hooked through the gills & strung up
to the western horizon. We are one,

burning with belief till the thing
inside the cage whimpers

& everything crazes out to a flash
of silver. Begged into the fat juice
of promises, our embrace is a naked
wing lifting us into premonition
worked down to a sigh & plea.

How It Is

My muse is holding me prisoner.
She refuses to give back my shadow,
anything that clings to a stone or tree
to keep me here. I recite dead poets
to her, & their words heal the cold air.
I feed her fat, sweet, juicy grapes,
& melons holding a tropical sun
inside them. From here, I see only
the river. The blue heron dives,
& always rises with a bright fish
in its beak, dangling a grace note.
She leans over & whispers, Someday,
I'll find some way to make you cry.
What are her three beautiful faces
telling me? I peel her an orange.
Each slice bleeds open a sigh.
Honeydew perfumes an evening
of black lace & torch songs,
& I bow down inside myself
& walk on my hands & knees
to break our embrace, but can't
escape. I think she knows
I could free myself of the thin gold chain
 invisible around her waist,
but if she left the door open,
I'd still be standing here
in her ravenous light.
Her touch is alchemical.
When she questions my love,
I serve her robin's eggs
on a blue plate. She looks me in the eye
& says, You still can't go. Somehow,

I'd forgotten I'm her prisoner,
but I glance over at the big rock
wedged against the back door.
I think she knows, with her kisses
in my mouth, I could walk on water.

Allegorical Seduction

I am piled up so high
in your walk, I
slide down a chute of years.
Touch me, mountains
rise, & the pleasure
tears us into a song.
Quicksilver skies, these birds
over The Four Corners
down through Gallup & Window Rock
catch fire in clouds.
No god tells them
different. No hand
disclaims our closing
distance, as doors open
under the sea.

— for Linda G.

Letter to Bob Kaufman

The gold dust of your voice
& twenty-five cents
can buy a cup of coffee.
We sell pain for next to nothing! Nope,
you don't know me but your flesh-
&-blood language lingers in my head
like treason & raw honey.
I read *GOLDEN SARDINE*
& dance the Calinda
to come to myself.
Needles, booze, high-steppers
with dangerous eyes.
Believe this, brother,
we're dice in a hard time hustle.
No more than handfuls of meat.
C'mon, play the dozens,
you root worker & neo-hoodooist,
you earth lover & hole-card peeper.
We know roads dusty with old griefs
& hot kiss joys.
Bloodhounds await ambush.
Something, perhaps the scent
of love, draws them closer.

Slam, Dunk, & Hook

Fast breaks. Lay ups. With Mercury's
Insignia on our sneakers,
We outmaneuvered to footwork
Of bad angels. Nothing but a hot
Swish of strings like silk
Ten feet out. In the roundhouse
Labyrinth our bodies
Created, we could almost
Last forever, poised in midair
Like storybook sea monsters.
A high note hung there
A long second. Off
The rim. We'd corkscrew
Up & dunk balls that exploded
The skullcap of hope & good
Intention. Lanky, all hands
& feet . . . sprung rhythm.
We were metaphysical when girls
Cheered on the sidelines.
Tangled up in a falling,
Muscles were a bright motor
Double-flashing to the metal hoop
Nailed to our oak
When Sonny Boy's mama died
He played nonstop all day, so hard
Our backboard splintered.
Glistening with sweat,
We rolled the ball off
Our fingertips. Trouble
Was there slapping a blackjack
Against an open palm.
Dribble, drive to the inside,

& glide like a sparrow hawk.
Lay ups. Fast breaks.
We had moves we didn't know
We had. Our bodies spun
On swivels of bone & faith,
Through a lyric slipknot
Of joy, & we knew we were
Beautiful & dangerous.

We Never Know

He danced with tall grass
for a moment, like he was swaying
with a woman. Our gun barrels
glowed white-hot.
When I got to him,
a blue halo
of flies had already claimed him.
I pulled the crumbled photograph
from his fingers.
There's no other way
to say this: I fell in love.
The morning cleared again,
except for a distant mortar
& somewhere choppers taking off.
I slid the wallet into his pocket
& turned him over, so he wouldn't be
kissing the ground.

Birds on a Powerline

Mama Mary's counting them
Again. Eleven black. A single
Red one like a drop of blood

Against the sky. She's convinced
They've been there two weeks.
I bring her another cup of coffee

& a Fig Newton. I sit here reading
Frances Harper at the enamel table
Where I ate teacakes as a boy,

My head clear of voices brought back.
The green smell of the low land returns,
Stealing the taste of nitrate.

The deep-winter eyes of the birds
Shine in summer light like agate,
As if they could love the heart

Out of any wild thing. I stop,
With my finger on a word, listening.
They're on the powerline, a luminous

Message trailing a phantom
Goodyear blimp. I hear her say
Jesus, I promised you. Now

He's home safe, I'm ready.
My traveling shoes on. My teeth
In. I got on clean underwear.

No Love in This House

Tonight I touch your breasts.
September's fruit.
Nipples, eyes of fire.
I kiss you deep
as a knife could go.

I pull you out of your jeans.
Black panties, red rose,
my fingers find
the center of you
where the blues begin.

I'm in a room of you
where a white horse
shockwaves. It's hard to break
away: flesh, wine, language.
We curve into dance.

When I drive myself into you
you're singing the name
of a man in Rifle Gap
with his cowboy boots propped
on another woman's kitchen table.

The Thorn Merchant

When he enters the long room
more solemn than a threadbare Joseph coat,
the Minister of Hard Knocks & Golden Keys
begins to shuffle his feet.
The ink on contracts disappears.
Another stool pigeon leans
over a wrought-iron balcony.
While men in black wetsuits
drag Blue Lake, his hands dally
at the hem of his daughter's skirt.

In the brain's shooting gallery
he goes down real slow.
His heart suspended in a mirror,
shadow of a crow over a lake.
With his fingers around his throat
he moans like a statue
of straw on a hillside.
Ready to auction off his hands,
he knows how death waits
in us like a light switch,
& there are teeth marks
on everything he loves.

Longitudes

Before zero meridian at Greenwich
Galileo dreamt Dante on a ship
& his beloved Beatrice onshore,
both holding clocks, drifting apart.

His theory was right even if
he couldn't steady the ship
on rough seas beyond star charts
& otherworldly ports of call.

"But the damn blessed boat
rocked, tossing sailors to & fro
like a chorus of sea hags
in throes of ecstasy."

My whole world unmoors
& slips into a tug of high tide.
A timepiece faces the harbor–
a fixed point in a glass box.

You're standing on the dock.
My dreams of you are oceanic,
& the Door of No Return
opens a galactic eye.

If a siren stations herself
between us, all the clocks
on her side, we'll find each other
sighing our night song in the fog.

The Piccolo

"There's Ayisha,"
you say, pointing to a wall
yellowing with snapshots
& theatre posters, her face
wakes Piaf & Lady Day
on the jukebox, swelling this
12 x 12 room. A voice
behind the espresso machine
says Ayisha's in town,
& another says No,
she's back in New York.
Everyone's like Ehrich
Weiss in a tiger cage,
a season to break
things & make ourselves
whole. Someone puffs a J
rolled in perfumed paper,
& in my head I'm scribbling
you a love note, each word
sealed in amber. A cry
seethes from a semi-dark
corner, hidden like potato
eyes in a root cellar. My lips
brush your right cheek.
It's St. Valentine's Day,
but there's no tommy gun
in a violin case from Chicago
because it is your birthday.
You buy another sweet
for me, & when I take a bite
I taste desire. Another
dollar's dropped into the box:

Bud Powell's "Jor-Du"
fills The Piccolo,
& we move from one truth
to the next. Fingers
on the keys, on the spine.
Passion & tempo. We kiss
& form the apex that knows
what flesh is, the only
knot made stronger
by time & pressure.

Canticle

Because I mistrust my head & hands, because I know salt
    tinctures my songs, I tried hard not to touch you
even as I pulled you into my arms. Seasons sprouted
    & went to seed as we circled the dance with silver cat bells
tied to our feet. Now, kissing you, I am the arch-heir of second chances.
    Because I know twelve ways to be wrong
& two to be good, I was wounded by the final question in the cave,
    left side of the spirit level's quiver. I didn't want to hug you
into a cross, but I'm here to be measured down to each numbered bone.
    A trembling runs through what pulls us to the blood knot.
We hold hands & laugh in the East Village as midnight autumn
    shakes the smoke of the Chicago B.L.U.E.S. club from our clothes,
& you say I make you happy & sad. For years I stopped my hands
    in midair, knowing fire at the root stem of yes.
I say your name, & another dies in my mouth because I know how to plead
    till a breeze erases the devil's footprints,
because I crave something to sing the blues about. Look,
    I only want to hold you this way: a bundle of wild orchids
broken at the wet seam of memory & manna.

Nothing Big

The hummingbird's rainbow
        lands among red
                geraniums.

God's little hell-rising
  helicopter flies away,

& I'm back in Danang.
  Was the rich boy's cocaine
                this good

or have I been trying years
to return to this hard night

of mahogany trees shadowing men
back from a firefight? The sun
strikes broken glass on the ground
& triggers dancing lights in my head—
the sky's flesh wounds.
            I'm back at the Blue Dahlia
            lying beside someone I can't

forget.

Inside me a flurry of wings
stirs up trouble,
& I'm lifting off.

The Heart's Graveyard Shift

I lose faith in my left hand
not because my dog Echo's eloped
with ignis fatuus into pinewoods
or that my limp's unhealed
after 13 years. What can go wrong
goes wrong, & between loves an empty
space defines itself like a stone's weight
helps it to sink into earth.
My devil-may-care attitude
returns overnight, the bagwoman
outside the 42nd Street Automat
is now my muse. I should know
by heart the schema, routes
A & B, points where we
flip coins, heads or tails,
to stay alive. Between loves
I crave danger; the assassin's cross hairs
underline my point of view.

                            Between loves,
with a pinch of madness tucked under
the tongue, a man might fly off the handle
& kill his best friend over a penny.
His voice can break into butterflies
just as the eight ball cracks
across deep-green felt,
growing silent with something unsaid
like a mouth stuffed with nails.
He can go off his rocker, sell the family
business for a dollar, next morning
pull a Brink's job & hijack a 747.
He can hook up with a woman in silver

spike heels who carries a metallic blue guitar
or he can get right with Jesus
through phenobarbital.

                              Between loves
I sing all night with the jukebox:
"Every man's gotta cry for himself."
I play chicken with the Midnight Special
rounding Dead Man's Curve, enthralled
by the northern lights & machinery
of falling stars. Internal solstice,
my body, a poorly rigged by-pass
along Desperado Ave., taking me away
from myself. Equilibrium's whorehouses.
Arcades scattered along the eastern seaboard.
I search dead-colored shells for clues,
visions, for a thread of meat,
untelling interior landscapes.
A scarecrow dances away with my shadow.
Between loves I could stand all day
at a window watching honeysuckle open
as I make love to the ghosts
smuggled inside my head.

After Summer Fell Apart

I can't touch you.
His face always returns;
we exchange long looks
in each bad dream
& what I see, my God.
Honey, sweetheart,
I hold you against me
but nothing works.
Two boats moored,
rocking between nowhere
& nowhere.
A bone inside me whispers
maybe tonight,
but I keep thinking
about the two men wrestling nude
in Lawrence's *Women in Love.*
I can't get past
reels of breath unwinding.
He has you. Now
he doesn't. He has you
again. Now he doesn't.

You're at the edge of azaleas
shaken loose by a word.
I see your rose-colored
skirt unfurl.
He has a knife
to your throat,
night birds come back
to their branches.
A hard wind raps at the door,
the new year prowling

in a black overcoat.
It's been six months
since we made love.
Tonight I look at you
hugging the pillow,
half smiling in your sleep.
I want to shake you & ask
who. Again I touch myself,
unashamed, until
his face comes into focus.
He's stolen something
from me & I don't know
if it has a name or not—
like counting your ribs
with one foolish hand
& mine with the other.

Sugar

I watched men at Angola,
How every swing of the machete
Swelled the day black with muscles,
Like a wave through canestalks,
Pushed by the eyes of guards
Who cradled pump shotguns like lovers.
They swayed to a Cuban samba or Yoruba
Master drum & wrote confessions in the air
Saying *I been wrong*
But I'll be right someday.
I gazed from Lorenzo's '52 Chevy
Till they were nighthawks,
& days later fell asleep
Listening to Cousin Buddy's
One-horse mill grind out a blues.
We fed stalks into metal jaws
That locked in sweetness
When everything cooled down & crusted over,
Leaving only a few horseflies
To buzz & drive the day beyond
Leadbelly. At the bottom
Of each gallon was a glacier,
A fetish I could buy a kiss with.
I stared at a tree against dusk
Till it was a girl
Standing beside a country road
Shucking cane with her teeth.
She looked up & smiled
& waved. Lost in what hurts,
In what tasted good, could she
Ever learn there's no love
In sugar?

Lover

A turning away from flowers.
A cutting out of
stone understands, naked
before the sculptor.

I watch you down Telegraph Avenue
till you sprout into a quivering
song color.

But I hope you fall
from your high horse
& break your damn neck.

Excerpt from *Love in the Time of War*

Tonight, the old hard work of love
has given up. I can't unbutton promises
or sing secrets into your left ear
tuned to quivering plucked strings.

No, please. I can't face the reflection
of metal on your skin & in your eyes,
can't risk weaving new breath into war fog.
The anger of the trees is rooted in the soil.

Let me drink in your newly found river
of sighs, your way with incantations.
Let me see if I can't string this guitar

& take down your effigy of moonlight
from the cross, the dogwood in bloom
printed on memory's see-through cloth.

My Father's Love Letters

On Fridays he'd open a can of Jax
After coming home from the mill,
& ask me to write a letter to my mother
Who sent postcards of desert flowers
Taller than men. He would beg,
Promising to never beat her
Again. Somehow I was happy
She had gone, & sometimes wanted
To slip in a reminder, how Mary Lou
Williams' "Polka Dots & Moonbeams"
Never made the swelling go down.
His carpenter's apron always bulged
With old nails, a claw hammer
Looped at his side & extension cords
Coiled around his feet.
Words rolled from under the pressure
Of my ballpoint: Love,
Baby, Honey, Please.
We sat in the quiet brutality
Of voltage meters & pipe threaders,
Lost between sentences . . .
The gleam of a five-pound wedge
On the concrete floor
Pulled a sunset
Through the doorway of his toolshed.
I wondered if she laughed
& held them over a gas burner.
My father could only sign
His name, but he'd look at blueprints
& say how many bricks
Formed each wall. This man,
Who stole roses & hyacinth

For his yard, would stand there
With eyes closed & fists balled,
Laboring over a simple word, almost
Redeemed by what he tried to say.

Sitting in a Rocking Chair,
Going Blind

the exact
          second
       the lights come on
     like the aurora borealis
i'm sitting at a window of summer
          for two weeks   waiting for
       a pomegranate tree
       to fall & scatter
   fruit on the ground
      on the corner
       a black buick
          special
             runs down a child
          like 40 brass cymbals
          & 40 tambourines
       the air coagulates
       in the background
       a bright bird
       falls from the sky
       its scream is black
   a dog drops dead
pissing on a fire hydrant
     a woman's dance   burns off
       with a green flame
          anemones
       spray the air white
     in a world of dark
i can only remember to put my hands all over you

Anodyne

I love how it swells
into a temple where it is
held prisoner, where the god
of blame resides. I love
slopes & peaks, the secret
paths that make me selfish.
I love my crooked feet
shaped by vanity & work
shoes made to outlast
belief. The hardness
coupling milk it can't
fashion. I love the lips,
salt & honeycomb on the tongue.
The hair holding off rain
& snow. The white moons
on my fingernails. I love
how everything begs
blood into song & prayer
inside an egg. A ghost
hums through my bones
like Pan's midnight flute
shaping internal laws
beside a troubled river.
I love this body
made to weather the storm
in the brain, raised
out of the deep smell
of fish & water hyacinth,
out of rapture & the first
regret. I love my big hands.
I love it clear down to the soft
quick motor of each breath,

the liver's ten kinds of desire
& the kidney's lust for sugar.
This skin, this sac of dung
& joy, this spleen floating
like a compass needle inside
nighttime, always divining
West Africa's dusty horizon.
I love the birthmark
posed like a fighting cock
on my right shoulder blade.
I love this body, this
solo & ragtime jubilee
behind the left nipple,
because I know I was born
to wear out at least
one hundred angels.

Yusef Komunyakaa is a professor and senior distinguished poet in the graduate Creative Writing Program at New York University. He is the author of twenty books of poetry, including *Neon Vernacular,* for which he won the Pulitzer Prize and the Kingsley Tufts Poetry Prize. He is the recipient of numerous awards for his contributions to poetry, including the Wallace Stevens Award, the Ruth Lilly Poetry Prize, and the Griffin Prize Lifetime Recognition Award.

Oliver Egger is a poet, editor, and journalist based in New Haven, CT. He was selected as a 2023 CT State Student Poet and edited and compiled *The Route 9 Anthology* (Wesleyan, 2022).

Poems in this chapbook originally appeared in the following books:

-Dedications & Other Dark Horses (R.M.C.A.J. Books, 1977): "Allegorical Seduction"

-Lost in the Bonewheel Factory (Lynx House Press, 1979): "Corrigenda", "For You, Sweetheart, I'll Sell Plutonium Reactors", "No Love in This House", "Sitting in a Rocking Chair, Going Blind"

-Copacetic (Wesleyan, 1984): "Copacetic Mingus", "Letter to Bob Kaufman"

-I Apologize for the Eyes in My Head (Wesleyan, 1986): "Unnatural State of the Unicorn", "The Thorn Merchant", "The Heart's Graveyard Shift", "After Summer Fell Apart"

-Toys in a Field (Black River Press, 1986): "Nothing Big"

-Dien Cai Dau (Wesleyan, 1988): "We Never Know"

-*Magic City* (Wesleyan, 1992): "Banking Potatoes", "Slam, Dunk, & Hook", "Sugar", "My Father's Love Letters

-*Neon Vernacular: New and Selected Poems* (Wesleyan, 1993): "Birds on a Powerline"

-*Thieves of Paradise* (Wesleyan, 1998): "The Piccolo", "Anodyne"

-*Talking Dirty to The Gods* (Farrar, Straus and Giroux, 2001): "Euphony"

-*Pleasure Dome: New and Selected Poems* (Wesleyan, 2004): "Reminiscence", "Providence", "Lover"

-*The Chameleon Couch* (Farrar, Straus and Giroux, 2011): "How It Is", "Canticle"

-*Love in the Time of War* (Robin Price, Printer & Publisher, 2013): "Excerpt From *Love in the Time of War*"

-*The Emperor of Water Clocks* (Farrar, Straus and Giroux, 2015): "Longitudes"

Wesleyan Chapbooks

Entanglements by Rae Armantrout

Notice by Rae Armantrout

The Poetry Witch Little Book of Spells by Annie Finch

I Will Teach You About Murder: 29 Love Poems, edited by
Shea Fitzpatrick, Sallie Fullerton and Torii Johnson

Deaths of the Poets by Kit Reed, Illustrated by Joseph W.
Reed

Dog Truths by Kit Reed, Illustrated by Joseph W. Reed

Thirty Polite Things to Say by Kit Reed, Illustrated by
Joseph W. Reed

Printed in the USA
CPSIA information can be obtained
at www.ICGtesting.com
LVHW051201150724
785214LV00007B/14

9 780819 501677